HOW IT WORKS
TELEVISIONS

by Rachel Hamby

WWW.FOCUSREADERS.COM

Focus Readers is distributed by North Star Editions:
sales@northstareditions.com | 888-417-0195

Produced for Focus Readers by Red Line Editorial.

Content Consultant: Robert J. Thompson, Director, Bleier Center for Television and Popular Culture, Syracuse University

Photographs ©: Andrey Popov/iStockphoto, cover, 1; bonetta/iStockphoto, 4–5; Ann Ronan Picture Library Heritage Images/Newscom, 7; Red Line Editorial, 8; IxMaster/Shutterstock Images, 10–11; monkeybusinessimages/iStockphoto, 13; Sean Pavone/Shutterstock Images, 15; Vertigo3d/iStockphoto, 16–17; jakkapan21/iStockphoto, 19; marcociannarel/iStockphoto, 21; scyther5/iStockphoto, 22–23; ttsz/iStockphoto, 25; Sorbis/Shutterstock Images, 26–27; sdominick/iStockphoto, 29

ISBN
978-1-63517-237-9 (hardcover)
978-1-63517-302-4 (paperback)
978-1-63517-432-8 (ebook pdf)
978-1-63517-367-3 (hosted ebook)

Library of Congress Control Number: 2017935886

Printed in the United States of America
Mankato, MN
June, 2017

ABOUT THE AUTHOR

Rachel Hamby was born in Utah, the same state where the inventor of the electronic television was born. Now she lives in Spokane, Washington, where she watches television with her husband and a corgi that loves nature programs. She also writes poems and stories for kids.

TABLE OF CONTENTS

CHAPTER 1

INSPIRATION AND INVENTION

Every day, millions of people pick up their remotes and watch their favorite shows. But few understand the science taking place behind the screen.

A TV is actually part of a system that sends and receives video and audio information. First, the information is broken down into electronic signals.

For a TV set to work, it must receive sound and picture information.

Then the signals are sent out. Finally, a **receiver** picks up the signals and turns them back into sound and images.

Inventors of the TV were inspired by radio technology. Because sound could be transmitted over the air without wires, they wondered if pictures could be transmitted, too. John Logie Baird built the first TV system in 1926. It used two spinning discs. Glass lenses around the first disc picked up light from the object. The light hit a **photoelectric cell**. This cell changed the light energy into electric signals.

The signals were sent by wire to a receiver. The receiver used a second

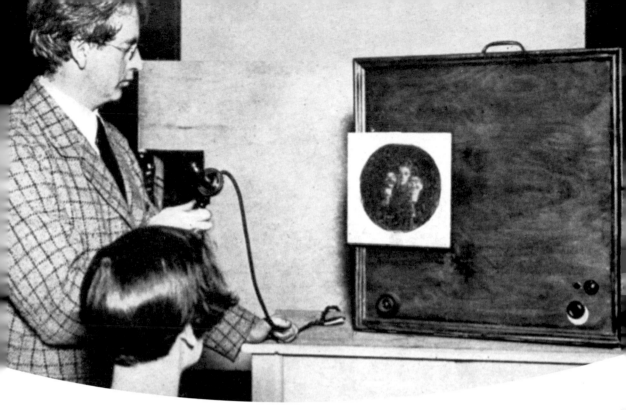

The first TV images were not very clear and often flickered.

spinning disc to create an image of the object. It used a process called scanning. Starting at one corner, the disc created one line of the image at a time.

Philo T. Farnsworth made the first electronic TV in 1927. His TV system used cathode rays instead of spinning discs.

A cathode ray is a beam of **electrons** that is made inside a vacuum tube. The electronic TV system had one cathode ray tube in the camera. Another tube was in the receiver. To make an image, a cathode ray in the camera picked up light from the object. Then a cathode ray in the receiver reassembled the image. The ray hit a glass screen at the end of the tube.

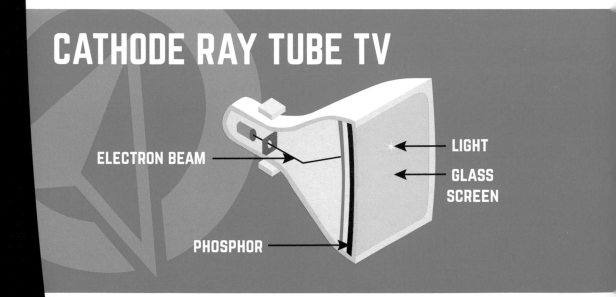

CATHODE RAY TUBE TV

ELECTRON BEAM

LIGHT

GLASS
SCREEN

PHOSPHOR

The screen was coated in phosphor. The phosphor made the screen light up when it was hit by the ray. The ray scanned one row of the image at a time.

For several years, TVs only displayed black-and-white images. In the 1950s, inventors made a system to broadcast colors, too. Color TVs used three electron beams. One beam was red. One was green. The third was blue. Together, the beams scanned an image onto the screen. The three colors blended together. This made a full range of colors in the image.

By 1972, more color TVs were sold than black-and-white TVs. Since then, TVs have continued to improve.

CHAPTER 2

SENDING SIGNALS

Sound and picture information is sent to a TV as a signal. To create signals, cameras and microphones capture light and sound. At first, TVs used **analog** signals. A camera split each image into a series of electrical impulses. The impulses created a signal, which varied depending on how bright the light was.

Places where TV cameras record programming are called studios.

Dark areas of the image made weak electrical impulses. Bright areas made strong impulses.

Microphones picked up sound to go with the images. They changed the sound into electrical impulses, too. These impulses created a signal that varied depending on the sound's pitch.

TV stations broadcast these signals. An antenna on the station's transmission tower sent the signals out on radio waves. The radio waves traveled through the air. Antennas on viewers' roofs picked up the radio waves. Then the antennas sent the radio waves to the viewers' TVs.

With just a TV receiver and antenna, viewers can watch programs on many channels for free.

In 2009, US broadcasts switched to digital signals. This method encodes the image and sound into **bits**. Each bit represents a small part of the image or sound. Like analog signals, digital signals are sent out over radio waves.

However, digital signals can carry more information over longer distances. They provide clearer pictures and sound, too.

Signals can also be sent through cords or cables. Cable TV companies use coaxial cables to bring signals to people's homes. Devices such as DVD players might use other cables, such as HDMI cables. These connect into ports on the back of the TV. This brings the signal from the device to the TV.

Some TVs get signals from satellites. A dish on or near the viewer's home picks up the signals. Cables then carry the signals from the dish to the TV. Other TVs

Satellite dishes are often placed on roofs.

can **stream** signals by connecting to the Internet.

Viewers select different options on the TV's menu. This allows them to switch between a broadcast, a streamed Internet program, or another device.

CHAPTER 3

TUNING IN

A TV receives signals and changes them back into light and sound. Each TV channel has a specific **frequency**. The **tuner** finds the radio wave that matches the selected channel. Then, the tuner removes the digital audio and video signals from the radio wave.

A tuner can pick up many different kinds of programs.

These signals are still encoded. The tuner decodes the signals. The signals are turned back into electrical charges.

Next, the tuner sends the video signals to the video circuit board. From there, the signals are sent to the screen, where the electrical energy is turned back into light. The tuner sends the audio signals to the audio circuit board. This circuit board sends the signals to the speakers. The speakers turn the signals back into sound.

CRITICAL THINKING

Why do the digital signals need to be decoded before they are sent to the video and audio circuit boards?

A circuit board contains many small electronic parts.

The tuner also syncs the video and audio information. This makes the pictures and sound play together. Finally, the tuner formats the video to fit the size of the TV screen.

REMOTE CONTROL

A remote control sends coded signals to a TV. The signals can perform actions such as changing the channel, controlling the sound, and turning the TV on or off. Inside a remote control is a circuit board. The circuit board is a thin piece of fiberglass with copper wires etched onto the surface. For each button on the remote, there is a disk on the circuit board. This disk can conduct electricity.

When a person presses the remote's button, a connection is made between the button and the disk. This connection sends an electrical charge. The charge travels down a copper wire to an electronic circuit called a chip. The chip produces a code specific to that button. It sends the code to an infrared light-emitting diode (LED). The

A remote control also allows viewers to access the TV's menu.

infrared signal is sent to the TV. It tells the TV which function to perform.

CHAPTER 4

BEHIND THE SCREEN

The images on a TV screen appear to be moving. But they are actually a series of individual images. Each image is slightly different. By displaying the images very quickly, a TV tricks viewers' eyes into seeing a moving picture.

Flat-screen TVs use small dots known as pixels to create each image.

Some LCD TVs can display more than 16 million colors.

Each image is made up of many rows of pixels. Each pixel contains three subpixels. One is red. One is green. The third is blue. Together, they can create a wide variety of colors.

In liquid crystal display (LCD) TVs, liquid crystals are arranged in a grid of columns and rows. The crystals are between layers of electrodes. Two polarizing filters control the type of light waves that pass through. The filters cause the light waves to follow a specific pattern.

To light up a particular pixel, the electrodes send a charge down a column and a row. The charge travels through the liquid crystals. It causes the crystals to twist. This allows light to pass through a pixel and the filter. Changing the charge's strength controls how bright the light is.

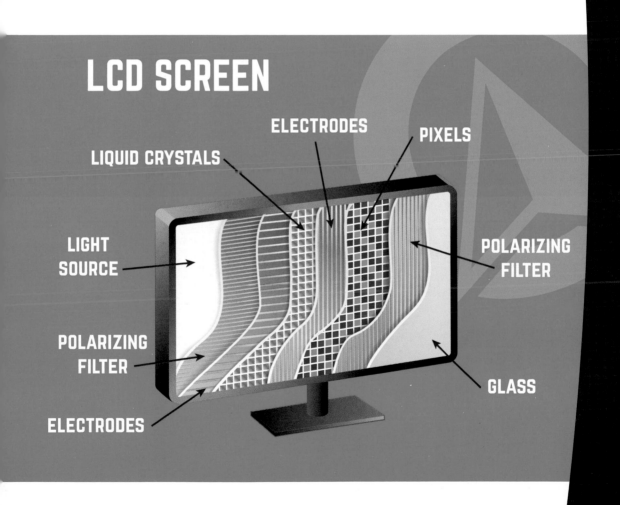

LCD SCREEN

LIQUID CRYSTALS

ELECTRODES

PIXELS

LIGHT SOURCE

POLARIZING FILTER

POLARIZING FILTER

GLASS

ELECTRODES

CHAPTER 5

IMPROVING QUALITY

High-definition TVs (HDTVs) were introduced in the late 1990s. Their wide displays imitated the screens used in movie theaters. This new shape allowed HDTVs to show a wider angle of an image. HDTVs also had more pixels in their screens. As a result, they could display clearer, more detailed pictures.

Ultra-HDTV screens can have more than 8 million pixels.

27

Today, Ultra-HDTVs use even more pixels. They display even higher-quality images.

Showing more images per second helps TVs imitate lifelike movement. Older TVs display 25 to 30 images each second. But newer TVs can display up to 120 images per second.

A smart TV combines a TV set with a computer. Viewers connect smart TVs to the Internet. Then, they can stream programs, play games, use apps, and much more.

Smart TVs can even connect to users' smartphones.

Companies can also make 3D TVs. These TVs display two images at once. Viewers wear special glasses. The glasses cause each eye to see a slightly different image. This makes the images seem to have depth. Some companies are working to make 3D TVs that work without glasses. They are known as Ultra-D TVs. People continue designing TVs to display sharper, clearer pictures.

FOCUS ON
TELEVISIONS

Write your answers on a separate piece of paper.

1. Write a sentence that explains the main idea of Chapter 2.

2. Would you rather have a 3D TV or a smart TV? Why?

3. What part decodes the signals into information a TV can display?

    A. the antenna
    B. the speaker
    C. the tuner

4. What would happen if the electrodes in a TV screen did not send an electrical charge through the liquid crystals?

    A. Sound would not come out of the speakers.
    B. Light would not go through the pixels.
    C. Signals would not be received by the antenna.

Answer key on page 32.

GLOSSARY

analog
Measuring or representing data by using a continuously changing signal instead of by using numbers.

bits
Units of information in computing and digital communication. Each bit has a value of zero or one.

electrons
Charged particles that can be in atoms or on their own.

frequency
The number of cycles per second that a radio wave has.

photoelectric cell
A device that generates an electric current whose strength depends on the brightness of the light hitting it.

receiver
A device that picks up and converts radio waves or other signals.

stream
To send or receive a steady flow of data.

tuner
The part of a TV that converts radio waves back to audio and video signals.

TO LEARN MORE

BOOKS

Laine, Carolee. *Inventing the Television*. Mankato, MN: The
Child's World, 2016.

Otfinoski, Steven. *Television: From Concept to Consumer*.
New York: Children's Press, 2015.

Spilsbury, Richard, and Louise Spilsbury. *The Television*.
Chicago: Heinemann Library, 2012.

NOTE TO EDUCATORS

Visit **www.focusreaders.com** to find lesson plans,
activities, links, and other resources related to this title.

INDEX

Answer Key: 1. Answers will vary; **2.** Answers will vary; **3.** C; **4.** B

CAPSTONE PRESS
a capstone imprint

by
THOM STORDEN

The Refrigerator, Prime Time,
Touchdown Tom, and More!

FOOTBALL'S
GREATEST
NICKNAMES

Sports Illustrated KIDS

Capstone Captivate is published by Capstone Press, an imprint of Capstone.
1710 Roe Crest Drive
North Mankato, Minnesota 56003
capstonepub.com

SPORTS ILLUSTRATED KIDS is a trademark of ABG-SI LLC. Used with permission.

Library of Congress Cataloging-in-Publication Data is available
on the Library of Congress website.
ISBN: 9781663906915 (hardcover)
ISBN: 9781663920492 (paperback)
ISBN: 9781663906885 (ebook pdf)

Summary: Many of the greatest football players have earned funny, odd, or interesting nicknames during their careers. Read to find out the stories behind football's legendary nicknames.

Image Credits
Associated Press: Greg Trott, bottom right 23, Paul Spinelli, 28; Getty Images: Bettmann, 26; Newscom: Everett Collection, 19; Shutterstock: Mtsaride, (football) Cover, Tiwat K, (doodles) design element throughout; Sports Illustrated: Andy Hayt, 18, David E. Klutho, top 23, Erick W. Rasco, 4, 6, 8, 14, 16, 17, Heinz Kluetmeier, 20, John Iacon, 10, 11, 24, Neil Leifer, 9, 12, 13, 25

Editorial Credits
Editor: Erika L. Shores; Designer: Terri Poburka; Media Researcher: Morgan Walters; Production Specialist: Laura Manthe

All internet sites appearing in back matter were available and accurate when this book was sent to press.

All records and statistics in this book are current through the 2020 season.

TABLE OF CONTENTS

Words in **BOLD** are in the glossary.

Patrick Mahomes is called the Kansas City Cannon. The nickname combines his team's city and the strength of his throwing arm.

Nicknames of the Gridiron

Football is fun. **Linebackers** and defenders chase running backs. Quarterbacks and wide receivers play catch. Touchdowns are celebrated with end zone dances and high fives. The players battle through rain, wind, mud, cold, and snow. With a sport like that, you know there will be some great nicknames.

Early on, players like "The Galloping Ghost" Red Grange and Elroy "Crazylegs" Hirsch ruled the **gridiron**. Today, it's TD slingers like "Touchdown" Tom Brady and Patrick "Kansas City Cannon" Mahomes. The next great football nickname is just a touchdown away.

Pigskin Fact

Where did the name "pigskin" come from? Early footballs were made of pig, cow, or other animal bladders stuffed with straw. People started referring to the balls as "pigskins." Today's footballs are made of cow leather and a special rubber.

CHAPTER 1

The Quarterbacks

Tom Brady led the Patriots for 20 seasons. No other NFL quarterback has played for the same team for that many seasons.

Quarterbacks take the snap. From there, they hand off, throw, or run the football. They are often the first players cheered for wins. They are also often the first player blamed for losses. It makes sense that quarterbacks are some of the most-often nicknamed players in football.

TOM BRADY:
Touchdown Tom

The better a player is, the more nicknames he often has. This is true for star quarterback Tom Brady. He's known as Touchdown Tom, Tom Terrific, TB12, The Pharaoh, or just Sir. Brady won a **record** six Super Bowls with the New England Patriots. Following the 2020 season, Brady added another big win. He won his seventh Super Bowl ring playing for the Tampa Bay Buccaneers.

Pigskin Fact

Tom Brady was drafted in the sixth round of the NFL Draft in 2000. He was the 199th player chosen.

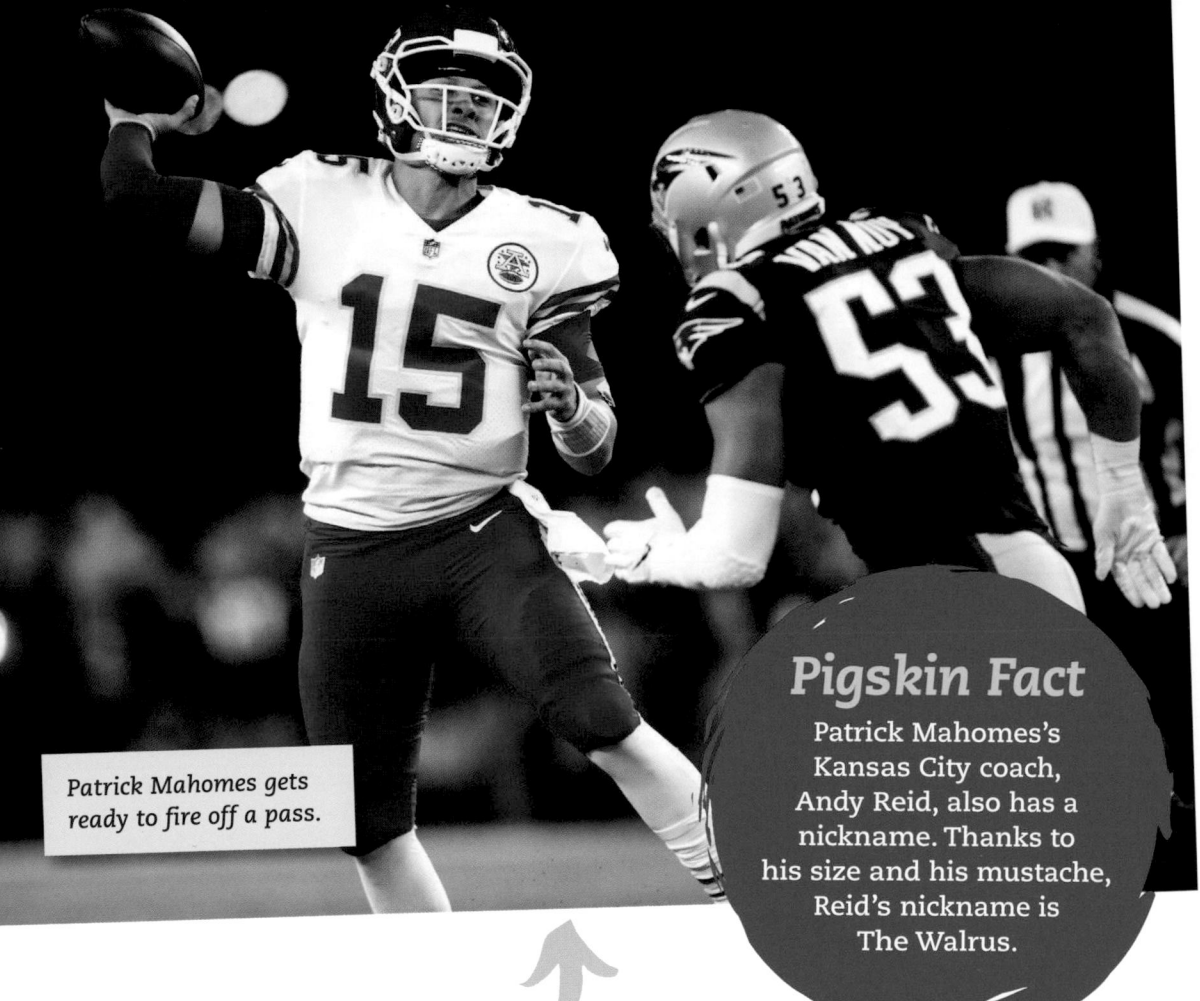

Patrick Mahomes gets ready to fire off a pass.

PATRICK MAHOMES:
Kansas City Cannon

Patrick Mahomes led the Kansas City Chiefs to a Super Bowl victory following the 2019 season. At age 24, Mahomes was named Super Bowl Most Valuable Player (MVP). Even at a young age, he's earned a lot of nicknames. Kansas City Cannon, Showtime, and Magic Man are just a few. Quarterbacks who can really fire off a long pass are said to have a "cannon" for an arm.

RYAN FITZPATRICK:
Fitzmagic

In the first 16 years of his NFL career, Ryan Fitzpatrick played for eight different teams. Along the way, he has thrilled fans with fourth-quarter comebacks and amazing plays. For his abilities to lead come-from-behind rallies, he was given the nickname Fitzmagic. In his career, he has led 18 game-winning drives.

STEVE "Air" MCNAIR

Tennessee Titans QB Steve McNair had a strong arm. When he aired out a deep pass, the football really flew. Air McNair played in the mid-1990s and early 2000s. That is when NBA basketball star Michael "Air" Jordan really shined. It was high praise to be called "Air" at that time.

"Broadway Joe" NAMATH

"Broadway Joe" Namath's looks and style made his fans think he belonged on a stage or movie screen. The New York Jets star passer won the 1968 league MVP and led his team to a Super Bowl win. A picture of him on the cover of *Sports Illustrated* magazine helped him get his nickname.

Joe Namath was a star NFL QB from 1965 to 1977.

FROM THE GRIDIRON TO THE SCREEN

Joe Namath did end up working as an actor. Namath was nominated for a Golden Globe Award for his role in the 1970 film *Norwood*. He won a TV Land Award for playing himself on *The Brady Bunch* in 1969.

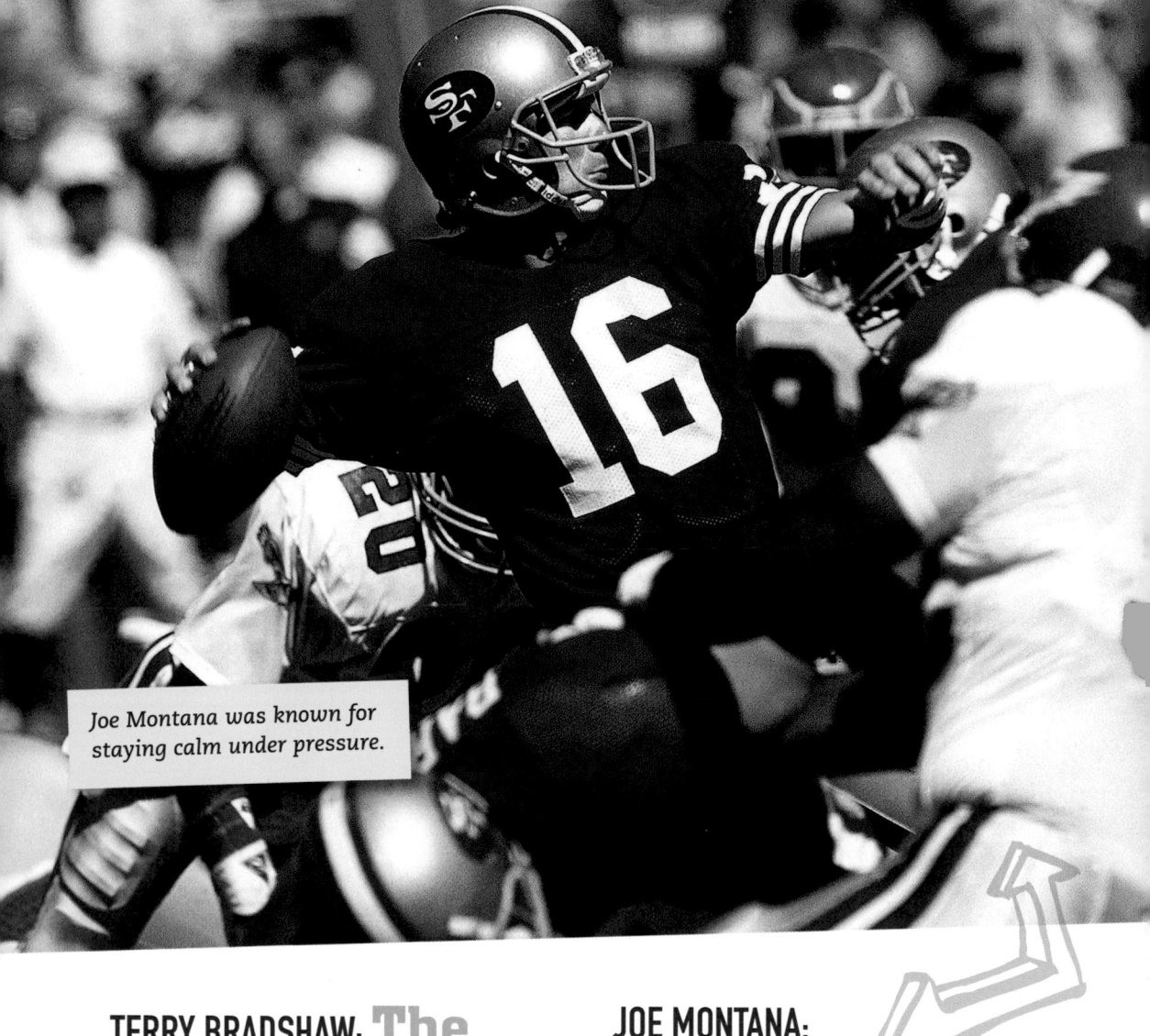

Joe Montana was known for staying calm under pressure.

TERRY BRADSHAW: The Blond Bomber

A football pass that spirals far and long is called a bomb. That's what the football looks like as it travels downfield through the air. Before sportscaster Terry Bradshaw lost his hair, he was blond and a standout quarterback. And he was a standout quarterback. The Blond Bomber won four Super Bowls in the 1970s as leader of the Pittsburgh Steelers.

JOE MONTANA: Joe Cool

Joe Montana won four Super Bowls with the San Francisco 49ers in the 1980s. The QB was a cool and calm leader. Once, in the huddle of a last-minute Super Bowl drive, Montana pointed out a famous actor in the stands. Teammates couldn't believe Montana wasn't more worried about the play on the football field!

DAN MARINO:
Dan the Man

Fans love a fun, rhyming nickname. During his NFL career, Dan "The Man" Marino was the big cheese in Miami. Marino led the Dolphins to the Super Bowl in 1985. In 17 seasons, he threw 420 touchdowns. It was the most ever at the time he retired.

JIM MCMAHON:
Mad Mac

Off the field, QB Jim McMahon always wore sunglasses and rode a motorcycle. On the sidelines, he wore headbands and argued with coaches. His Chicago Bears teammates and fans loved bad boy Mad Mac. A popular movie at the time called *Mad Max* likely sparked the nickname.

Jim McMahon's headbands helped him to stand out on the sidelines.

Pigskin Fact

Jim McMahon wore sunglasses for a reason. His eyes were bothered by bright light. As a kid, he had an accident involving one of his eyes.

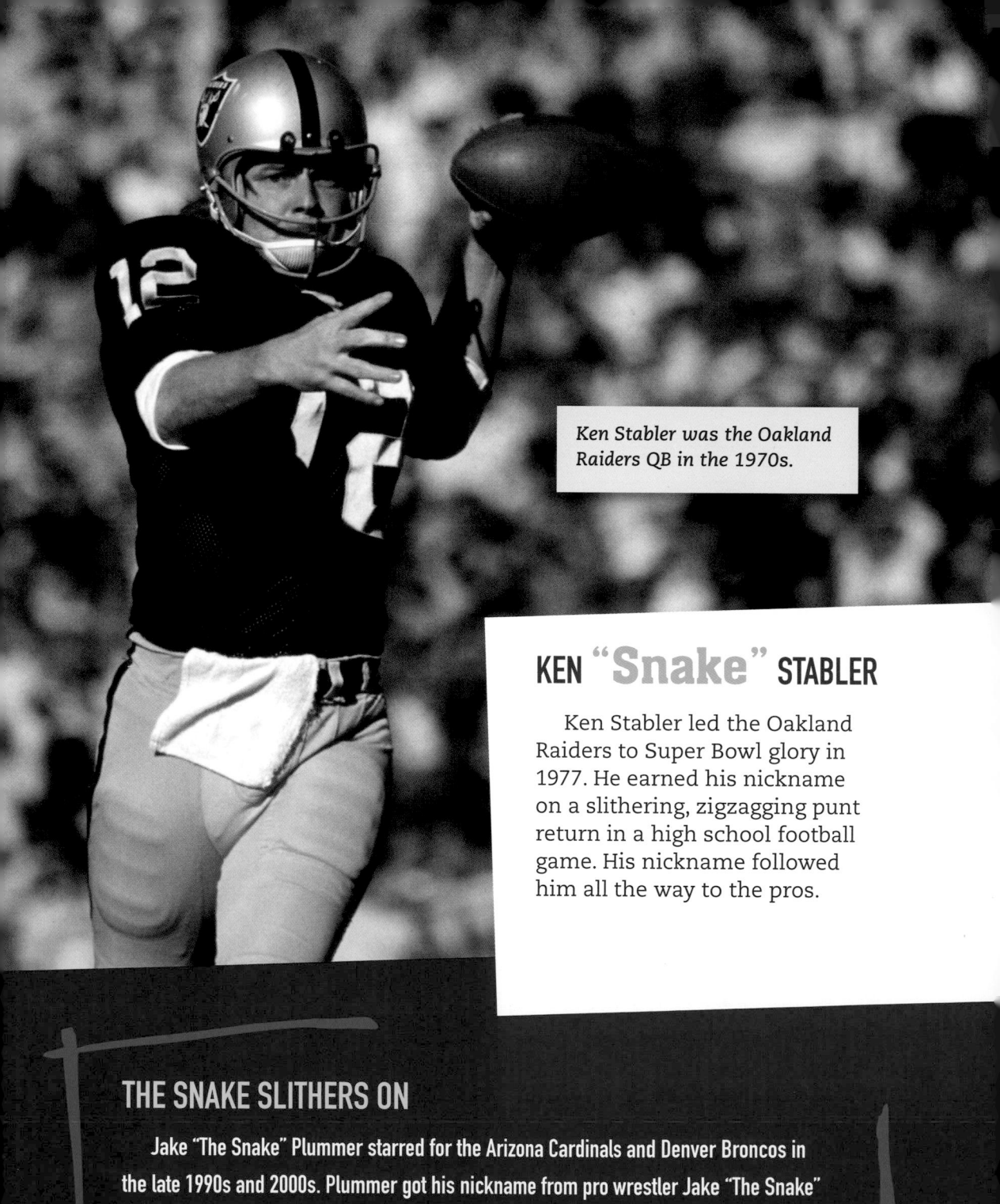

Ken Stabler was the Oakland Raiders QB in the 1970s.

KEN "Snake" STABLER

Ken Stabler led the Oakland Raiders to Super Bowl glory in 1977. He earned his nickname on a slithering, zigzagging punt return in a high school football game. His nickname followed him all the way to the pros.

THE SNAKE SLITHERS ON

Jake "The Snake" Plummer starred for the Arizona Cardinals and Denver Broncos in the late 1990s and 2000s. Plummer got his nickname from pro wrestler Jake "The Snake" Roberts. Roberts took his own nickname from Ken "Snake" Stabler, his childhood hero.

ROGER STAUBACH:
Captain Comeback

Roger Staubach was a star quarterback in the 1970s. Captain Comeback led many last-minute wins for the Dallas Cowboys. Possibly the most famous was a 1975 **Hail Mary** touchdown pass. That play allowed the Cowboys to beat the Minnesota Vikings and go to the Super Bowl. His nickname came from the way he led his team from behind to earn wins.

Roger Staubach fires off a pass during a 1971 playoff game.

Best of the Rest:
Other Great QB Nicknames

Matt Ryan: **Matty Ice**

Peyton Manning: **The Sherriff**

Norman **"Boomer"** Esiason

Fran Tarkenton: **The Mad Scrambler**

Daryle Lamonica: **The Mad Bomber**

Johnny Unitas: **Johnny U**

Y.A. Tittle: **The Bald Eagle**

"Slingin'" Sammy Baugh

CHAPTER 2

The Touchdown Makers

Rob Gronkowski played for the Patriots for nine seasons.

The touchdown makers in football earn six points per end zone visit. Often times the running back, wide receivers, and tight ends are the ones scoring the touchdowns. These players have also earned some great nicknames.

ROB GRONKOWSKI: Gronk

Some nicknames are simple and easy to remember. Rob "Gronk" Gronkowski has one of those names. Gronk spent much of his career catching Tom Brady–thrown TDs as the New England Patriots' star tight end. Fans remember how he helped the team to two Super Bowl wins. He and Brady teamed up again in Tampa Bay in 2020, where they went on to win the Super Bowl.

MARSHAWN LYNCH: Beast Mode

When Marshawn Lynch took the handoff, fans said he went into "beast mode." Lynch ran over linebackers. He stiff-armed cornerbacks and crashed into safeties. In 2013 and 2014, Lynch led the NFL in **rushing** touchdowns as a Seattle Seahawk.

LARRY FITZGERALD: Fitz

Few recent wide receivers have put up stats like Larry Fitzgerald. His high number of receptions and touchdowns have led to 11 Pro Bowls in 17 years with the Arizona Cardinals. Fitzgerald has said opponents call him Fitz because he gives them fits. The defenders who have tried to stop Fitzgerald might agree.

GRONKS ALL AROUND

Rob Gronkowski has three brothers who also made it to the NFL. His oldest brother, Dan, played tight end for the Lions, Broncos, Browns, and Patriots. His next-oldest brother, Chris, played running back for the Cowboys, Colts, and Broncos. His youngest brother, Glenn, was a running back for the Patriots.

Travis Kelce helped Kansas City win the Super Bowl following the 2020 season.

Pigskin Fact

Travis Kelce's brother, Jason, also plays in the NFL. He was drafted in 2011 to play center for the Philadelphia Eagles.

TRAVIS KELCE: Zeus

Kansas City Chiefs fans love it when their team scores. Quite often it's tight end Travis Kelce doing the scoring. Kelce's fans call him Zeus. He's strong and powerful like the king of the Greek gods. Kelce scored a career-best 11 touchdowns in the 2020 season.

CALVIN JOHNSON: Megatron

Calvin Johnson was the greatest receiver in Detroit Lions history. Johnson had a lanky frame and huge hands. He could leap and stretch for catches over smaller defensive backs. Lions receiver Roy Williams gave Johnson his Megatron nickname. Williams thought Johnson looked like the huge Transformers character.

JEROME BETTIS:
The Bus

When Jerome Bettis lined up in the backfield, he was ready to roll. For 13 seasons, The Bus rumbled through the line, dragging would-be tacklers along for the ride. Over his career, Bettis gained 13,662 yards and scored 91 touchdowns. He drove the Pittsburgh Steelers to the Super Bowl title following the 2005 season.

STEFON DIGGS:
Diggsy

"Diggsy" is a play on Stefon Diggs's last name. Diggs joined the Buffalo Bills in 2020 and led them to the playoffs.

Diggs is known for a catch with a nickname of its own. In the 2018 playoffs, Diggs caught a pass and scored a game-winning touchdown for the Minnesota Vikings. That play, which occurred at the Vikings home stadium, is known as the "Minneapolis Miracle."

Stefon Diggs led the NFL with 127 receptions in 2020.

Walter Payton leaps over a line of defenders during a game.

WALTER PAYTON:
Sweetness

Walter Payton was one of the smoothest ballcarriers to ever strap on football cleats. He had the footwork of a dancer and the speed of an Olympic runner. It's not certain how he got the nickname Sweetness. Some say it was first used when he played college football. Some say it was because of his high-pitched voice. Some say it was because he was kind and helpful off the field.

RED GRANGE: **The**
Galloping Ghost

Red Grange was a college football star for Illinois. In a 1924 game against Michigan, Grange romped for four touchdowns in the first half. This was against a Michigan team that had allowed only two touchdowns in the two previous years. As a result, Warren Brown, a Chicago sportswriter, gave Grange the nickname The Galloping Ghost. Grange later played for the Chicago Bears.

PAUL HORNUNG:
The Golden Boy

Paul Hornung was a standout at the University of Notre Dame before he became a Green Bay Packers star. The speedy running back was nicknamed in part for his blond hair. It didn't hurt that he won college football's golden Heisman Trophy.

. . . .

ELROY "Crazylegs" HIRSCH

Elroy Hirsch got his nickname from the way he ran. Hirsch's legs seemed to go in different directions at once. But Crazylegs was a great receiver. In 1951 the Los Angeles Rams player led the league in receiving and scoring.

BEST OF THE REST:
Other Great Touchdown Maker Nicknames

"**Bullet**" Bob Hayes

Daryl "**Moose**" Johnston

Billy "**White Shoes**" Johnson

Andre "**Bad Moon**" Rison

Raghib "**Rocket**" Ismail

DeAndre Hopkins: **Nuk**

Red Grange carries the ball down the field.

A POEM FOR THE GALLOPING GHOST

When Brown called Red Grange The Galloping Ghost, fellow sportswriter Grantland Rice wrote this poem.

A streak of fire, a breath of flame
Eluding all who reach and clutch;
A gray ghost thrown into the game
That rival hands may never touch;
A rubber bounding, blasting soul
Whose destination is the goal.

CHAPTER 3

The Defenders

William Perry played eight full seasons with the Chicago Bears.

Football defenders are big and quick. They block. They tackle. They rush quarterbacks. They do what they can to stop the other team from scoring. And some of the best defenders end up with some of the best nicknames.

WILLIAM "The Refrigerator" PERRY

William Perry stood 6-foot-2 (188 centimeters) and weighed 335 pounds (152 kilograms). He was big, like a refrigerator. Fans loved calling him The Fridge.

Perry was more than an awesome defensive tackle. In 1985 he scored three touchdowns in the regular season. He capped it off with another rushing TD in that season's Super Bowl for the champion Chicago Bears. Most defensive linemen spend their careers never scoring a single touchdown.

Pigskin Fact

William "The Refrigerator" Perry wasn't the only member of his family to play in the NFL. His brother Michael Dean Perry spent 10 years in the league, the same number of years as his older brother.

J.J. WATT: J.J. Swat

Quarterbacks and running backs look out for J.J. Watt when he lines up across from them. That's because "J.J. Swat" is there to bat down passes. Watt played for the Houston Texans for ten seasons before signing with the Arizona Cardinals in 2021.

Watt is one of three brothers to make the NFL. T.J. Watt plays defense like his oldest brother J.J. His middle brother, Derek, is a running back.

TYRANN MATHIEU: Honey Badger

While at Louisiana State University, Tyrann Mathieu earned his unique nickname. Thanks to his dyed blond hair and his tough attitude, he was called Honey Badger. Injuries early in his first pro season almost ended his career. But Mathieu's grit helped him work his way back. He won a Super Bowl with the Kansas City Chiefs following the 2019 season.

DEION SANDERS: Prime Time

One of the NFL's great defensive backs was Deion Sanders. He received his Prime Time nickname after scoring 30 points in a high school basketball game. Prime Time had a knack for playing his best when the game was on the line. In the mid-1990s, he won back-to-back Super Bowls. The first was with the 49ers. The next year he won with the Cowboys. Sanders had many other nicknames, including Neon Deion and Leon Sandcastle.

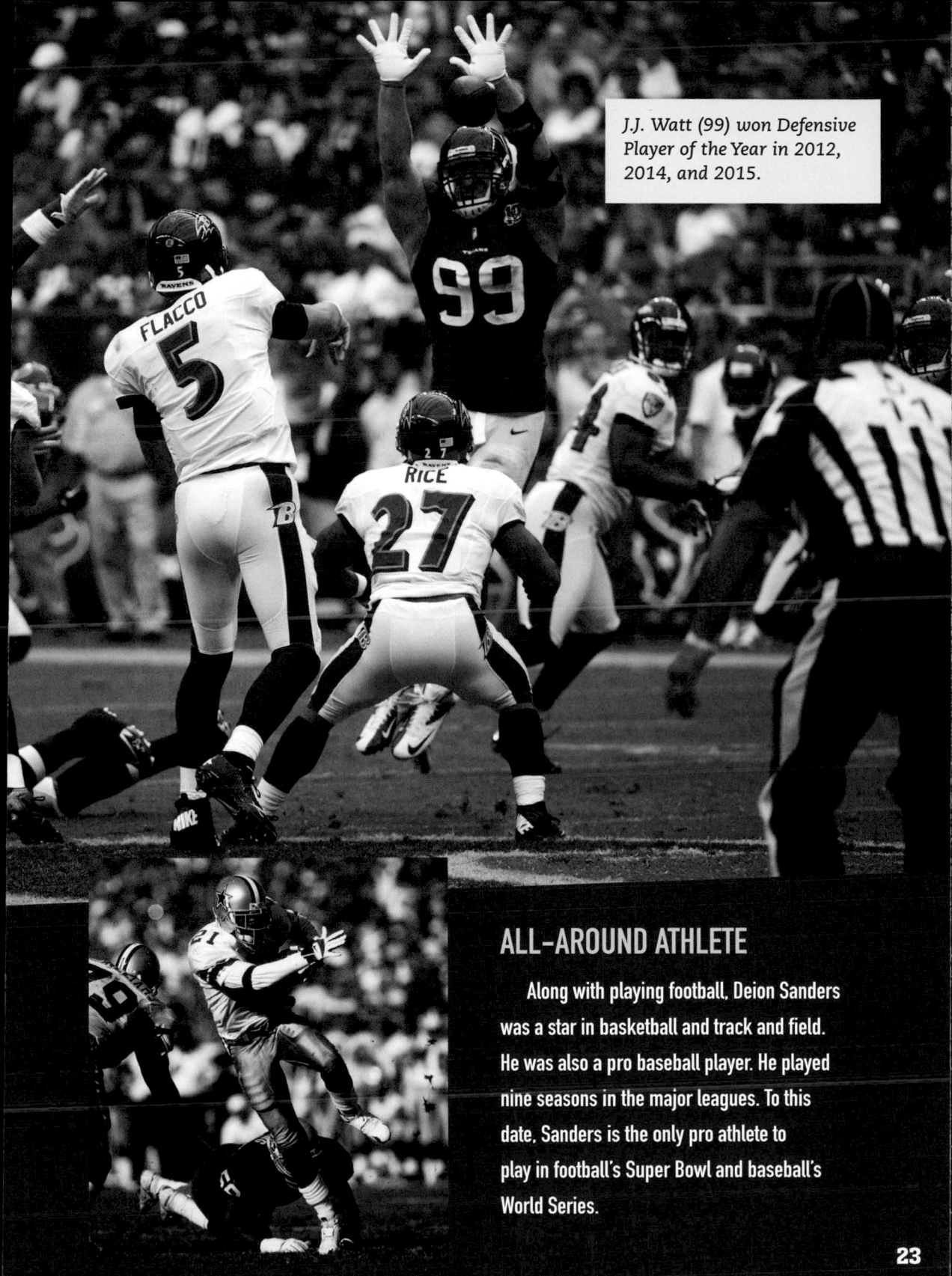

J.J. Watt (99) won Defensive Player of the Year in 2012, 2014, and 2015.

ALL-AROUND ATHLETE

Along with playing football, Deion Sanders was a star in basketball and track and field. He was also a pro baseball player. He played nine seasons in the major leagues. To this date, Sanders is the only pro athlete to play in football's Super Bowl and baseball's World Series.

Reggie White led the NFL in sacks in the 1987 and 1988 seasons as a member of the Philadelphia Eagles.

ED "Too Tall" JONES

Ed "Too Tall" Jones looked like he belonged on the basketball court. The 6-foot-9 (206 cm) defensive end stood out as a Dallas Cowboy. In 1979 "Too Tall" Jones retired and sat out the season after five years in the NFL. The following year, he came back and played 10 more seasons.

REGGIE WHITE:
The Minister of Defense

The Philadelphia Eagles were blessed when Reggie White became a star in the late 1980s. A church minister, White went on to play for the Green Bay Packers. He helped them win a Super Bowl. He also would play for the Carolina Panthers. White was voted into the Hall of Fame in 2006.

"Mean" JOE GREENE

"Mean" Joe Greene got his nickname in college. Mean Green was the nickname of the football team he played for at North Texas State University. Greene went on to star with the Pittsburgh Steelers. He was voted NFL Defensive Player of the Year in 1972 and 1974.

LAWRENCE TAYLOR: L.T.

Just two letters could strike fear into quarterbacks. Lawrence Taylor was known as L.T. Taylor was a threat to quarterbacks for 13 seasons with the New York Giants. Out of those 13 seasons, he made it to the Pro Bowl 10 times.

Joe Greene (#75) was a member of the "Steel Curtain" defense in Pittsburgh.

BEST OF THE REST: Other Great Defensive Player Nicknames

Darrelle Revis: **Revis Island**

Nate Newton: **The Kitchen**

Dick "**Night Train**" Lane

Alex Karras: **Mad Duck**

Bob Lilly: **Mr. Cowboy**

CHAPTER 4

The Wild and Weird

Ickey Woods (center) teaches his teammates the "Ickey Shuffle."

Some nicknames are weird. And sometimes it's not just players who get weird nicknames. Sometimes players' actions, such as touchdown dances, get nicknames. Sometimes it's a part of a team, such as the defense. Sometimes even the fans get nicknames.

"Ickey" WOODS

Elbert Woods's little brother couldn't say his big brother's name when they were young. It came out like "eeee eeee," which sounds like "Ickey." The nickname stuck. Every football fan knew it in 1988. That season, Woods was one of the NFL's leaders in rushing TDs. Fans loved watching him do the "Ickey Shuffle" dance when he reached the end zone.

MITCH TRUBISKY:
Mr. Biscuit

While at the University of North Carolina, quarterback Mitch Trubisky's coach called him Mr. Biscuit. The weird nickname was tasty enough to follow Trubisky into the pros.

Fans in the Dawg Pound are loyal to their Cleveland Browns team.

HaHa CLINTON-DIX

Ha'Sean Clinton-Dix got his nickname as a baby. His grandmother called him HaHa. She thought Clinton-Dix was a happy, giggly child. Years later, the nickname seemed fun and colorful when HaHa made it to the NFL.

TED HENDRICKS:
The Mad Stork

Ted Hendricks's long arms and legs caused his Raiders teammates to call him The Mad Stork. After 15 seasons, 26 **interceptions**, 16 fumble recoveries, and four Super Bowl rings, The Mad Stork flew into the Pro Football Hall of Fame.

The Dawg Pound

The Dawg Pound is the nickname of a section in the Cleveland Browns home stadium. Seats in the "Dawg Pound" are near the east end zone. These loyal fans dress up in Browns gear. They wear dog masks or costumes. Waving bones in the air, they woof and cheer for their team no matter the score.

Pigskin Fact

The Purple People Eaters helped the Vikings to four Super Bowls in the 1970s.

MINNESOTA VIKINGS:
The Purple People Eaters

In the 1970s, the Minnesota Vikings defensive line was tough. It seemed like running backs disappeared going into it. The Purple People Eaters nickname was born. Two members of this group, Carl Eller and Alan Page, made it to the Hall of Fame.

Football has exciting action and standout stars. Fans keep track of player and team stats. Amazing passes and crazy catches aren't soon forgotten. Football's greatest nicknames only add to the fun.

BEST OF THE REST: Great Team Nicknames

Pittsburgh Steelers: **The Steel Curtain**, after the great Steeler defenses of the 1970s

Dallas Cowboys: **America's Team**, named for drawing fans from all over the country

St. Louis Rams: **The Greatest Show on Turf**, named for the offense of the late 1990s and early 2000s

Rams Seattle Seahawks: **The 12th Man**, named for fans so loud they're like another player on the field

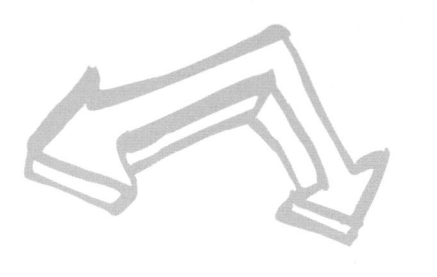

GLOSSARY

gridiron (GRID-eye-urn)—the football field

Hail Mary (HAYL MAY-ree)—a play where the quarterback throws the ball deep toward the end zone in the hope that one of the team's receivers will catch it

interception (in-tur-SEP-shun)—a pass caught by a defensive player

linebacker (LYN-bak-ur)—a player on the defending team whose usual position is a short distance in back of the line of scrimmage

record (REK-urd)—when something is done better than anyone has done it before

rushing (RUSH-ing)—the act of advancing a football by running plays; also, the yardage gained by running plays

sac (SAK)—when a defensive player tackles a quarterback who is attempting to pass the football

READ MORE

Chandler, Matt. *Football's Greatest Hail Mary Passes and Other Crunch-Time Heroics.* North Mankato, MN: Capstone Press, 2020.

Corso, Phil. *Patrick Mahomes.* New York: PowerKids Press, 2022.

Hewson, Anthony K. *Football Records.* Lake Elmo, MN: Focus Readers, 2021.

INTERNET SITES

Football: Player Positions
ducksters.com/sports/footballplayerpositions.php

NFL Players
nfl.com/players

Sports Illustrated Kids: Football
sikids.com/football

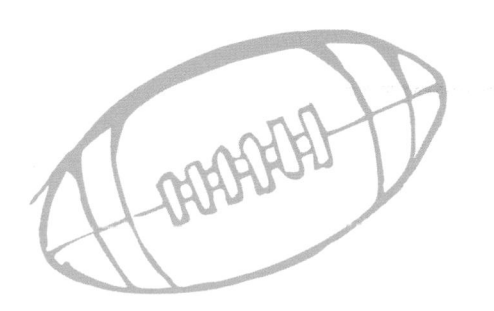

INDEX